T0393350

Published in 2022 by Enslow Publishing, LLC
29 East 21st Street, New York, NY 10010

Copyright © 2021 Booklife Publishing
This edition is published by arrangement with Booklife Publishing

Cataloging-in-Publication Data

Names: Wood, John, 1990-.
Title: Fierce fats / John Wood.
Description: New York : Enslow Publishing, 2022. | Series: Brain food | Includes glossary and index.
Identifiers: ISBN 9781978523883 (pbk.) | ISBN 9781978523906 (library bound) | ISBN 9781978523890 (6 pack) | ISBN 9781978523913 (ebook)
Subjects: LCSH: Lipids in human nutrition--Juvenile literature. | Nutrition--Juvenile literature.
Classification: LCC QP751.W66 2022 | DDC 613.2'84--dc23

Designer: Jasmine Pointer
Editor: William Anthony

Printed in the United States of America

CPSIA compliance information: Batch #CSENS22: For further information contact Enslow Publishing, New York, New York at 1-800-398-2504

Find us on

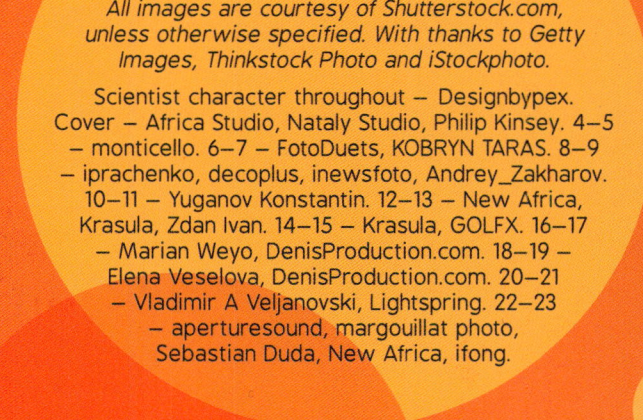

PHOTO CREDITS

FIERCE FATS

Written by
John Wood

Enslow
PUBLISHING

CONTENTS

Words that look like this can be found in the glossary on page 24.

A SLICE OF SCIENCE

Are you always being told you shouldn't eat more ice cream? Do you get told to eat more green vegetables? You might be wondering: why does it matter what I eat?

Hello!
I'm a small scientist. I'm here to teach you about food. Food is very important!

You might have heard the words "healthy diet." A diet is the kinds of food you usually eat. To have a healthy diet, you need to make sure you eat many different kinds of food.

A healthy diet is often called a **balanced** diet because you eat lots of different types of food.

PORTIONS

A portion, or serving, of food is the amount a person eats in one sitting. Sometimes they are <u>measured</u> in ounces.

You can use a food scale to weigh a portion of something in ounces.

A portion might be one orange.

The right portion size is different for every food. You should have five servings of fruits and vegetables a day. A serving of fruit is roughly the amount you can fit in the palm of your hand.

WHAT ARE FATS?

Fats are found in lots of foods. Our bodies need a certain amount of healthy fats to grow well.

Let's have a look at some foods full of good, healthy fats.

Tofu

8

Boiled soybeans

Peanut butter

Eggs

LET'S EXPERIMENT!

This mood bar will tell us about people's bodies. It shows four things — how tired they are, how healthy their skin is, how well they can <u>concentrate</u>, and how well they can see in <u>dim</u> light.

ENERGY

SKIN

CONCENTRATION

EYESIGHT

WAKE UP

She should eat some nuts! Let's try some almonds and Brazil nuts – they have plenty of fat in them. Your body uses fat as extra <u>energy</u>.

Brazil nuts

Almonds

13

SEEING CLEARLY

Avocado

Give him some avocado. Avocado is full of good, healthy fats. Fat helps the body take in <u>vitamins</u> including vitamin A, which helps you see in dim light.

ENERGY

SKIN

CONCENTRATION

EYESIGHT

THE FATS OF LIFE

Feed her fatty fish right now! The fat found in fish helps keep your skin healthy. It is also good for your heart and helps your blood to <u>clot</u> when it needs to.

Salmon is a type of fish that is full of these healthy fats.

RISE AND SHINE

Whole grain cereal

Wait – too much of some kinds of fats are bad for concentration! Let's change his breakfast. Give him <u>whole grain</u> cereal. This has vitamin B12, which is good for the brain. It will give him energy!

19

FOOD SWAPS

Some types of meat are fattier than others.

There are different types of fat. Some kinds of fat aren't good for the body. It's a good idea to only enjoy them sometimes.

Fast foods, like french fries and doughnuts, are nice to have as a treat every once in a while. But eating a variety of foods is important for a healthy body!

Many foods have fats in them! Here are just a few.

Sausages

Chocolate

Cake

Butter

22

THE MOST IMPORTANT THING

A certain amount of healthy fats is very good for you. However, don't forget that it is important to eat lots of different types of food. That is what makes a diet healthy and balanced.

Carbs

Fruits and vegetables

Protein

Fats and sugars

Dairy

23

GLOSSARY

balanced	made up of the right or equal amounts
clot	when blood thickens into a clump near a cut or wound so no blood flows out
concentrate	to give your attention to something
dim	without a lot of light
energy	the ability to do something
measured	to have found out the exact amount of something using units or systems, such as ounces for weight or feet for distance
vitamins	things that are found in food, which your body needs to work properly
whole grain	containing the whole of the grain seed and all the nutrients

INDEX